Ways into Science

Lifecycles

Written by Peter Riley

W
FRANKLIN WATTS
LONDON • SYDNEY

First published in 2003 by Franklin Watts
338 Euston Road, London NW1 3BH

Franklin Watts Australia
Level 17/207 Kent Street
Sydney, NSW 2000

Series editor: Sarah Peutrill
Art director: Jonathan Hair
Design: Ian Thompson
Photography: Ray Moller (unless otherwise credited)
Picture researcher: Diana Morris

A CIP catalogue record for this book
is available from the British Library

ISBN 978 0 7496 7678 0

Printed in Malaysia

Picture Credits:
Richard Anthony/Holt Studios p. 9b; Frank Blackburn/Ecoscene/Papilio p.
27cr; Nigel Cattlin/Holt Studios pp. 9t, 10l, 11t; Corbis p. 24l; Pat
Doyle/Corbis p. 23cr; Paul Franklin/Ecoscene/Papilio front cover & pp.16b,
18b; Daniel Heuchin/NHPA pp. 19, 27cl; Eric & David Hosking/Corbis p.
21; Ute Klaphake/Photofusion p. 24tr; Clariss Leahy/Photofusion p. 25b;
Michael Maconachie/Ecoscene/Papilio p. 13t; Ken Preston-
Mafham/Premaphotos p. 10r; Robert Pickett/Ecoscene/Papilio pp. 12t, 17,
18t, 22, 27c; Lynda Richardson/Corbis p. 20t; M.J.Thomas/FLPA p. 11b;
Roger Tidman/Corbis p 20b; Alan Towse/Ecoscene/Papilio p. 27tr; Bob
Watkins/Photofusion pp. 6, 7; Barrie Watts pp. 12b, 14, 27tl; Ken
Wilson/Ecoscene/Papilio pp. 13b, 15

Whilst every attempt has been made to clear copyright should there be
an inadvertent omission please apply in the first instance to the publisher
regarding rectification.

Thanks to our models:
Donna Perkin, Nicholas Porter, Pernell Lamar Simpson

To my granddaughter Megan Kate

Franklin Watts is a division of Hachette Children's Books.

Contents

What is a lifecycle?

All living things have a lifecycle. There are different stages in a lifecycle.

Many living things are born.

They grow.

They change.

They can
have young.

They grow old and
then die.

Plants

The lifecycle of a plant starts when its seed sprouts.

Tom has put some pea seeds in soil.

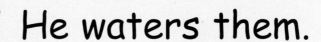

He waters them.

Soon seedlings grow out of the seeds.

The seedlings grow taller and become plants with leaves.

Tom plants them outside.

Buds grow.

What do you think the buds will grow into? Turn the page to find out.

Flowers and seeds

A flower grows out of each bud. Flowers make nectar for bees to feed on.

Flowers also make pollen. Bees carry it between the flowers as they feed on the nectar.

The pollen is needed to make seeds.

The seeds scatter and grow into new plants.

Some plants die after the flowers have made seeds.

Some can grow new flowers again next year.

Some trees live for thousands of years.

Ben has found some eggs on a leaf.

He looks at the eggs every day. One day he finds tiny caterpillars have hatched.

The caterpillars eat the leaves and grow.

When a caterpillar is fully grown it sheds its skin. It turns into a pupa (sometimes called a chrysalis).

What do you think happens next?
Turn the page to find out.

Inside the pupa
more changes
take place.

The pupa splits
open and a
butterfly
comes out.

The butterfly feeds on
nectar in flowers.

It lays some eggs. Soon after,
the butterfly dies.

What other animals change a lot in
their lifecycle? Turn the page to
find one example.

Amphibians

Amphibians change a lot in their lifecycle.

Emily has some frog spawn from a pond. It is made of frog eggs and jelly.

The eggs are black. The jelly is clear. You can see through it.

Emily looks at the frog spawn every day. One day she sees tadpoles hatching.

The tadpoles start to grow and change shape. They grow back legs.

Then they grow front legs.

What do you think happens next? Turn the page to find out.

Frogs

The tadpoles' tails shrink. They change into froglets.

The froglets leave the water and live on land.

In time they become frogs. In a few years they can make frog spawn too.

The lifecycle of a reptile starts with an egg.

When reptiles are fully grown, they lay eggs themselves.

What other creatures begin inside an egg? Turn the page to find one.

Birds

A bird starts life as an egg.

Chicks hatch out of the eggs.

The parents feed the chicks in the nest.

The chicks are soon ready to fly and feed on their own.

When they are grown they make nests and raise chicks themselves.

Mammals

Harry has a cat called Tibby.
Tibby has kittens.

The kittens feed on their mother's
milk. This helps them to grow.

Harry weighs each kitten every week. He records each weight.

He makes a chart of one kitten's growth. What do you think it will show?

The kittens will become adult cats after about 10 months.

Humans

Here are some stages in human life.

A baby sleeps a lot
and drinks milk.

Toddlers can walk
but often fall down.
Babies and toddlers need the
care of adults all of the time.

Children begin to learn how to look after themselves.

Adults can look after themselves and have children.

Which stage in the human lifecycle are you at?

What stage?

Look at the pictures opposite. What stage in a lifecycle does each picture show?

Make a table like this and fill it in.

Picture	starting out	growing up	having young
A			
B			
C			
D			
E			
F			
G			

A butterfly

B puppy

C reptile hatching

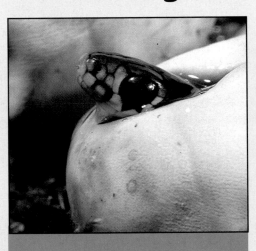

D tadpole,

E bird with nest

F seeds

G seedlings growing

27

 Useful words

adult – a fully grown person or animal.

amphibian – an animal such as a frog, toad or newt that has tadpoles in its lifecycle.

bird – an animal covered in feathers, with a pair of wings.

bud – a green lump on a stalk or twig. It can grow into a flower. Some buds grow into leaves and stems.

butterfly – an insect with two pairs of wings which are often brightly coloured.

egg - the first stage of animals. Most animals lay eggs but with some animals, such as mammals, the mothers keep the eggs inside their bodies and babies grow there.

flower – the part of a plant where seeds are made. Flowers come in all shapes, sizes and colours.

leaves – flat, usually green, parts of the plant.

milk – the liquid food baby mammals drink for some time after they are born.

nectar – a liquid that flowers make to attract bees.

pollen – a yellow dust made by flowers. It helps them to make seeds.

reptile – a group of animals with dry scaly skin. Lizards, snakes, tortoises and crocodiles are reptiles.

seed – plants start out as seeds.

seedling - a young plant that has just started to grow from the seed.

Some  answers

Here are some answers to the questions we have asked in this book. Don't worry if you had some different answers to ours; you may be right, too. Talk through your answers with other people and see if you can explain why they are right.

Page 23   The chart would show that the kitten's weight increases steadily until it is fully grown.

Page 25   You are probably at the children stage in the human lifecycle.

Page 26   A and E are 'Having young' (A is fully grown and ready to lay eggs). B, D and G are growing up. C and F are starting out. (Some animals develop inside eggs using the yolk for energy and materials to help it grow. Seeds also have a store of energy. Water is needed to make the tiny plant inside the seed grow and split the seed.)

Conservation note

Pages 16-18: The frog spawn was only removed from its pond for a short time so that a photograph could be taken. If spawn is collected a book on the care of tadpoles must be consulted so that you can give them the proper care while the children examine them. The tadpoles must be returned to water where their chances of survival are good. All activities involving the collecting and care of living things must be in accordance with school policies.

Index

About this book

Ways into Science is designed to encourage children to begin to think about their everyday world in a scientific way, examining cause and effect through close observation, recording their results and discussing what they have seen. Here are some pointers to gain the maximum use from **Lifecycles**.

• Working through this book will introduce the basic concepts about lifecycles and also some of the language structures and vocabulary associated with them. This will prepare the child for more formal work later in the school curriculum.

• On pages 9, 13, 15, 17, and 19 the children are invited to predict the change in the lifecycle of a living thing. Ensure that you discuss the reason for any answer they give in some depth before turning over the page. On page 9 look for an answer about flowers bursting out, but the children may also know about buds producing leaves. On page 13 look for an answer about a butterfly climbing out. On page 15 the children may say that people change. The butterfly and the frog provide examples of animals that have a complete change of form, not a more gradual change as seen in humans. On page 17 the children may say that the tadpole comes out of the water. On page 19 the children may refer to the butterfly so use the photographs to help prompt the children about birds.

• You may like the children to try Tom's activity on page 8. This can be linked to **Growing Plants**, another title in the **Ways into Science** series.

• You may like to enlist the help of a parent or carer to carry out Harry's activity on page 23 in the home of one of the children. The data collected can be used by the whole class to make a chart.